WITHDRAWN

D1029889

AN AUTHOR'S GUIDE TO RIGHTS REVERSION
AND PUBLISHING ON YOUR TERMS

TAKE
BACK
YOUR
BOOK

KATLYN   DUNCAN

First published August 2021, by Silent Storm Publishing

Cover designed by MiblArt

www.KatlynDuncan.com

ISBN-13: 978-1-954559-10-3

———

Publisher's Note: This work is drawn from the author's experience with rights reversion, and is meant to inspire and inform writers with tools and strategies to succeed in doing the same. The information in this book should be adopted to each individual's needs and goals for their books. As this book was published in 2021, the self-publishing information may change after publication.

Contents

Introduction

The dream for a lot of writers is to see their books on bookshelves. We want to spot readers posting beautifully curated photos on Instagram with glowing reviews and to hear how amazing our books are all across the internet.

That's all well and good, but, no pun intended here, books have shelf lives. Especially those published through a publishing house. The seasons of publishing with a large or small press turn over so quickly, and once your season has passed, then there's not much you can do for your book after that.

Or is there?

There are many clauses of a book contract that will affect your author career, but this guide is all about Rights Reversion.

Why?

It's a clause that can revive your book from the forgotten part of the shelf. Rights reversion allows you to grab that dusty baby of yours and clean it off for a whole new audience.

The best part is, you will finally take control over the entire process.

But I'm getting ahead of myself here.

Let's start with who I am, and why I'm so passionate about this topic.

My Journey

In 2009, I started taking my writing career seriously. I remember the moment my first book idea came into my head. I was walking through a parking lot and the story struck me like lightning. It was one of those unforgettable life-changing moments. I wrote this book during National Novel Writing Month (NaNoWriMo), which is an annual event held in November to finish a 50,000-word book within a month. I drafted that year, and several after, until I had a solid story. At this point, I was working full time in the medical field, and didn't put aside the time for my writing other than in November for a few years.

Shortly after NaNoWriMo 2012, there was a call for submissions for a new digital-first imprint of Harlequin UK. To caveat, I would never recommend submitting a book after NaNoWriMo, as most of the time a writer would have pushed through a first draft with little editing to "win". But this was my fourth iteration of the book, and it was in fairly good condition.

From that submission, the publisher reached out and I had a phone conversation with an editor. Ultimately, they loved the book and wanted a three-book series.

It was an absolute dream come true. I asked all the right questions, and it seemed like a perfect fit.

The three-book contract [Contract 1] landed in my

inbox, and I lived on Cloud Nine for weeks. I did my "due diligence" (notice the quotes here) and sent the contract to the lawyer who worked with us on selling our house (Mistake #1). I feel the winces and eye rolls. Hindsight is always 20-20. This lawyer did his best with the contract language, but as I came to realize, he didn't advise me of the nuances of a publishing contract, at least when it came to what exactly I was signing away. Proper knowledge about publishing is a must if you want to protect your books and career.

Fast forward to spring 2013, my debut novel, 'Soul Taken', the first in a series (*The Life After* series) of three young adult paranormal books, was out in the world. I was over the moon and had the debut author glow all the way through to the release of the last book in the series, which incidentally was less than a year later. Go digital-first publishing.

A note on digital-first publishing: This means the book will only come out in e-book to start. If the sales numbers skyrocket, the publisher may consider other formats (paperback, audio, etc.).

While I buried my head in drafting and editing the next two books, I thought everything would work out fine, because I had a publisher who was promoting my books (Mistake #2). If you don't already know, most publishers don't actively promote all the books on their lists the same. Unless you're a top title for the season, much of the promotion depends on you. Sure, there was the opportunity for social media posts and submissions to promotions that came later on (i.e. BookBub), but I had paid for my blog tour, book swag, and any other promotion for this series out of my pocket.

The next contract [Contract 2] came soon after, and my debut series would live on. Or so I thought.

My first brush with the idea of rights reversion was with the book I wrote while pregnant and then edited two months post-partum (again, digital-first publishing moves fast, but I would never recommend this for parents because lack of sleep doesn't make a great book). It absolutely tanked within the first few months of release.

When I caught up with my editor about the next book in the series, she suggested I move in a different direction with my genres. Instead of giving up, I asked for promotions to bring the book in front of new readers but was told that maybe the book would have sold better if it was in a different genre.

I'll let that settle in for a second.

She said *my book might have done better* (the book that was already published) *if it was in a different genre* (even though this book had gone through edits as a paranormal novel). To say I was dumbfounded was an understatement. This advice should have been given in the editing stage!

Can you tell I'm still a little bitter?

There's no use writing a book like this without honesty. For reference, that novel has sold under one hundred copies in its lifetime. It's an absolute failure.

No doubt the editor realized that and swiftly encouraged me to write contemporary novels with a dark twist.

I had another book and novella in this contract, so there was nothing I could do but move on.

This is where my writer friends came to the rescue. I learned that this wasn't an isolated incident. Books that didn't hit the mark in sales were left to die at the bottom of the book charts, but no one loved those stories as much as we did. We wanted to see them thrive, but we had signed away all control. What could we do?

One of those lovely humans informed me about rights reversion. Immediately, I flipped open my contract and found that buried treasure. I contacted the contracts department with a request to return this book to me at once! (Mistake #3).

I swear I was nicer than that.

The contracts department sent me a reply that I wasn't even close to the threshold amount of years that the book could fall under consideration of reversion, so there was nothing they could do.

How dare they, right?

That is a rhetorical question. Here's the hard truth. I signed this contract. My signature bound these terms to me and my books. I had to move forward, knowing that this book would fail, and there was nothing I could do about it.

A year later, when my contract ended, my editor informed me that young adult was no longer an age range that they were publishing. Which, in hindsight, probably assisted my process of rights reversion.

My young adult option book idea was rejected, and its subsequent adult-alternative, so I was contract-free for a bit. This was disheartening, but I saw it as an opportunity to get an agent and continue publishing my young adult thrillers.

A few months later, a new editor at that same imprint emailed me, asking if I was interested in writing a book about mermaids, as they were the new trend. Up to this point, I had been ghostwriting for a few years, so I saw this as an opportunity to collaborate. They gave me a three-novella deal [Contract 3]. I hired a literary lawyer who pointed out clauses that I should work to get altered. The main contention points for me were the option clause and keeping audio rights. As an author with no agent, I had a lot of push back from the publisher.

With those emails filled with refusals to my requests, I felt ungrateful. They had given me the opportunity to write these books, so what right did I have to ask to keep some sub-rights and change clauses?

It was the wrong mindset, which I know now. Books take a lot of time to conceive, write, edit, and promote. With digital-first publishing, most authors don't get an advance, and with my contract, I didn't see any royalties until at least three months post publication.

I signed the contract, and from that moment through to publishing the third novella (this took about a year to get them all out), both editors who wanted the books in the first place had left the imprint. My champions were gone, and I was thrust upon other editors who weren't as passionate about these books.

Can you guess what happened? Those books, again, tanked.

That new contract meant a new option clause (which is an entire book in itself), but basically means that the publisher has first refusal to my next similar book. These differ wildly across the board, but mine wouldn't allow me to publish unless I gave them the book to check out first. As young adult was no longer an option, I gave them an adult Christmas novel that had lived in my head for years.

They offered another two-book contract [Contract 4], and as I'd built up enough confidence (finally!) I asked to retain film rights, as Christmas movies aren't in short supply and the royalty that I would have to split was too high for my comfort. Sure, this is a pipe dream, but why not? As I expected, they pushed back. But you know what? I had nothing to lose at this point. I knew enough about contracts that even if I gave them the option book, I could still refuse a contract.

No one was more shocked than me when they agreed to let me keep those rights. Finally, a win, right?

At that point, I was energized to take control. So, when the first book in my debut series came up for reversion, I took it. This winning streak didn't quit as they decided to revert the entire series (even though the second and third books' rights hadn't expired).

Now, I had three books that I had full control over. They were and still are the books of my heart, and I had to get them back into the world, but this time, under my terms.

Once the books were down from all the retailers, I had to make a plan. I've never self-published before, and I wanted to research what others did.

This time, Google failed me. Okay, the search engine didn't, but I couldn't find more than a handful of articles — most from five or more years prior—about what authors did after reversion.

Did they republish these books?

Drawer them?

Give them away for free?

What?!

I suppose the basic information about rights reversion in those articles hasn't changed, but I wondered if there was more to this story. I asked as many authors as I could what they did after reversion, but I still wasn't satisfied. My wonder took me a on deep dive for months about what I should do for this series, and then this book (yes, the one you're reading right now) hit me again like a lightning bolt, and I knew from past experience I couldn't let it go.

Lessons learned from my mistakes

- Always have a lawyer/agent who is familiar with literary contracts review a contract prior to signing.
- Understand that unless you are one of the top books of the season, you will have to promote your book in some capacity.
- When asking for reversion prior to the threshold, you better have a solid argument for those rights, or you will have to be patient.

What to expect from this book

- A brief overview of rights reversion, and how to ask for those rights.
- Options for your book after reversion.
- Monetary considerations of republishing.
- Considerations for your author career as an independent or hybrid author.
- Success stories from authors who have had their rights reverted.

Success stories

As I mentioned, there wasn't a lot of tangible information out there on other's paths after rights reversion. So, I did my own research, and that involved asking writer friends if they knew anyone who had been in my position before, and also scouring online author groups for threads discussing this topic.

I found a few, and they are mentioned in this book. I am beyond grateful to those who have taken the time to share their story to help authors in similar situations. My hope for these interviews is that you connect with a story and find inspiration to keep your books alive.

Disclaimers and Definitions

I am not a lawyer.

While I have actively negotiated two of my four contracts, this guide doesn't contain legal advice for literary contracts. In my experience, the biggest thing I've learned is that unless you are a literary lawyer, always seek advice before signing anything.

Again, this is so important that it bears repeating. Ask for help whenever you don't understand something. Contract language is hard to read for someone who doesn't scour through it daily. Many authors think that a publisher has them and their book's best interests in mind, but they are a business. Do your due diligence, please.

Helpful resources I've found to assist authors get the best contract they can:

- Literary Agents: If you have an agent, discuss the publishing contract with them to make sure you understand all the clauses, and that they are to your liking.
- Authors Guild: Depending on your membership, you have access to lawyers who

are ready to review your contract, help with reversion of rights, give recommendations about changes, and so much more.

- Alliance of Independent Authors (ALLi): Similar to Author's Guild, with your membership you have access to general legal and business advice for contracts and more.
- Literary Lawyers: If you aren't interested in joining a society, you can hire a private lawyer. In this instance, you could search/ask author groups for recommendations. After doing research on them, make the best choice for you and always ask questions to ensure that you understand every single line of what you're signing away.

Publishers aren't bad.

My biggest hesitation in writing this guide was that readers would think I was a scorned author who hated publishers. This is not true at all.

This isn't a revenge story, but an empowering one. I have no plans to shut that door entirely, as I do believe that traditional publishing offers fantastic opportunities for some writers.

Typically, this route takes eighteen months to two years to get the book from contract to release (faster for most digital publishers), a significant amount of books fall out of favor within one season before they are replaced with the new and shiny. If you cannot continuously churn out bestsellers, the chances of making a living wage is slim. Which is why so many authors (whether or not they announce it) are doing freelance on the side, or taking a hybrid approach by self-publishing, to supplement the advance or royalty payments that may only come once (in the case of royalties) or quarterly (if you earned out your advance or have gone with a higher royalty structure with no advance).

Remember when I said that books that aren't sticky fall out of favor? It's not the publishers or the author's fault that one specific book didn't quite hit the mark for the net that was cast, but why not take control if your publisher isn't going to?

As I try to do with my advice to authors privately or on public platforms, I believe in honesty and protecting authors, and this is one way to protect your career and the books you've spent so much time with.

Definitions

There are so many variables with contracts or literary projects, but to make this guide simpler to follow, I'm defining a few terms:

Publisher - The Big 4 traditional publishers (Penguin/Random House, Hachette Book Group, HarperCollins, and Macmillan) aren't the only businesses out there who have contracts with reversion clauses. As you will see in the success stories, a myriad of options are available. So when I say publisher, that includes traditional, independent presses, small presses, hybrid publishers, basically any contract where the author signs away their rights to publish a book.

Book - any project that's been published whether it's a collection of poems, short stories, novellas, novels, etc.

. . .

Sub-rights – "Subsidiary rights" refer to offering the book in other media. This can include serial rights, translations, electronic books, audio recording, dramatization rights, book clubs, merchandising, other publications, etc.

Part I: Rights Reversion

Who is this book for?

Few authors publicly talk about what happens when their book isn't selling years after publication. Unless you are one of the one percent of household author names, your books will not live on without someone championing them.

That someone is you.

There are many clauses in a publishing contract that take control away from you, but I'm here to help you take it back if you are willing and able.

This is my hope for the words you're reading. I want to give you the options to breathe life into your book, take control of reaching more readers, and allow your book to thrive on your terms.

When brainstorming this book, I made myself the ideal reader. Well, me from years ago, at least. The author who was already in a contract and unsure what to do with her books that weren't selling a year past publication.

I also needed to write this book to the version of me before a contract.

Then, as long as I was going backward, I wanted to talk to the author who had completed and polished a novel and was looking at options for how to publish.

If you fit in any of these categories, or if you are interested in rights reversion at all, this book is for you.

The Contracted Author

If you are already in a contract, there's not much you can do right now, unless you're close to or past the reversion period. I'm the type of person who always needs to be prepared, so you aren't stuck, but you might have to wait to move on.

But that doesn't mean you can't prepare yourself for what you want to do with the book after you have the rights reverted.

I was in your shoes when my post-pregnancy book didn't sell, and I had to completely change my genre. It can be a lonely place when you realize that you're the only one who wants your book to succeed after your season is over. But all is not lost.

The Hopeful Contracted Author

Were you handed a contract, skimmed through the language, and stopped on the rights reversion clause? You, my dear hopeful, are at a tipping point in your career. You have a contract that has the opportunity to change your life. First of all, congrats!

Now, let's get to work.

Once upon a time, I was a publishing hopeful who took the first opportunity—without question—when someone presented it to me.

Bad, bad past-me.

While getting a publishing deal is an amazing and unexplainable thing, you are giving away a lot when you sign a contract. The validation from "the right people" is a thick fog over the fine print. Remember, a publisher is trying to get as much as they can from the deal as you are, so be sure you understand what that means for this book and your career.

The On-The-Fence Author

Has someone mentioned rights reversion to you in passing, or are you a successful independent author looking for more information about traditional publishing?

It's always good to know the pros and cons of both sides before making a choice. If you are already successful in the self-published market, you have a bit of leverage to decide what rights you're willing to give up to another entity. Weighing the risks is always important, and as I've said before, make sure the contract is 100% what you want before signing.

Even if you haven't published before, every book deserves consideration of its path. While I can't tell you where your book belongs (as this is completely up to you), I may be able to offer an idea on how to give your book the best shot it can have the first go-around

What is rights reversion?

Rights reversion gives you, the author, an opportunity to take back the book rights that you signed over to a publisher, after a period of time and meeting the thresholds within your contract.

The tricky thing about publishing now versus fifty years ago is the digital access to titles. Most contracts state that the book has to be "in print" for the publisher to retain these rights, but that definition includes digital e-books, and audio files along with actual print books (paperback, hardback, large print, etc.). This can sometimes hinder the author's ability to revert the rights when they want.

Then there is a threshold of time, monetary amount or units sold to consider. Contracts will usually stipulate an amount of time before publishers will consider reverting rights. Usually this is in years. They want to make as much money off their initial investment as possible, as any business would.

Example reversion language, "Income due to the Author from the sale or licensing of the Work is less than

$250 in any 12-month period no sooner than five years from the publication of the Work."

It's important to keep these dates and thresholds in mind the moment you have the inkling of an idea that you want your rights back. To prepare yourself, scour your royalty statements and track your sales every royalty period for this information.

What can rights reversion do for your book?

This is an important consideration. If you are happy to keep a book that isn't selling with a publisher, then that is your prerogative.

But, if you intend to have your book as a profitable product in your backlist, then you should think about all your options. As this process can sometimes be laborious, and possibly lead to legal action if all parties don't agree, you have to want this. It's a similar mindset to writing the book. You have to commit to it for it to become valuable to you, and rights reversion can be the same way.

How to get your rights reverted

The most common ways to get your book reverted to you is if both the reversion terms have expired and the threshold is fulfilled or if the publisher closes.

Fulfilled Option Clause

With my debut trilogy, I had to wait until the clause was fulfilled before becoming a successful reverted author.

Of the four contracts I signed, there were wild differences between all the reversion conditions. For perspective, I will be eligible for reversion for three of the books in my fourth contract before two of the books on my second.

As I mentioned, in this world of technology, the reversion clauses usually refer to the book being "in print". If your e-books and digital audiobooks are selling past the threshold, even if you're physical books aren't, then you most likely wouldn't have grounds to revert.

Your Publisher Closes

If your publisher is closing for any reason, or another company buys them, this may be an instance of exercising the right to revert your book. Check with your agent or contact at the publisher to inquire about the reversion. As this hasn't happened to me personally, fellow author, Maggie Wells, answers my questions and offers her experience.

Success Story: Maggie Wells

Margaret Ethridge/Maggie Wells is a hybrid author of contemporary romance and romantic suspense. You can find her at maggie-wells.com.

KATLYN: What type of publisher did you have your books reverted from?

MAGGIE: A digital-first imprint and from an independent/small press.

KATLYN: What was the process of rights reversion like for you?

MAGGIE: My small press publisher closed. The other titles were with the digital-first imprint of a larger publisher, and the term of my contract was up.

. . .

KATLYN: How did you get your rights back?

MAGGIE: With the small press, the owner promptly sent rights reversion letters to us for each title. They even gifted us the rights to any cover art they had created in house (with credit given) if we wished to reuse it. With the digital-first imprint, my sales were low, and the term had expired on two of the three books in one series, and all three in another. Of the series with the straggler, they reverted the first two, but refused to revert the third until the full three years had passed, regardless of the lack of sales. My agent handled the request, and it was fairly smooth, though I had a hard time getting them to remove titles from their own storefront.

KATLYN: After reversion, what plan did you have for this book?

MAGGIE: All of my books have been re-covered and released back into the wild. I have republished one three-book series already and plan to repackage and re-release the other this summer [2021].

KATLYN: What was the republishing process like? Did you use a pen name? Did you go through KDP Select or wide (all platforms)?

. . .

MAGGIE: I have experimented with KU [Kindle Unlimited], but at the moment, I am wide on all titles reverted. I have had one instance of rights pushback from Amazon on a particular title, despite sending the rights reversion letter to multiple customer service reps. In the end, I found that if I processed it without requesting a pre-order, it sailed right through.

KATLYN: What monetary expenses did you expect? Were there any surprises?

MAGGIE: I knew what to expect. I have paid for some re-editing and a few covers, but mostly I have done it on my own.

KATLYN: What is the best thing about having your rights reverted to you on this book?

MAGGIE: I can control my backlist promotion. I refuse to pay for advertisement on a book I don't own the rights to.

KATLYN: Any advice for authors who are going through rights reversion?

MAGGIE: Be patient, but persistent. Keep an eye on all outlets and make sure they have removed their version of the book before putting yours up. Most of all, don't be afraid to try new things with old titles (promote them, serialize, freebies, etc.) They are yours to play with. I have one title that's ten-years old that BookBub loves. Take time to find where each particular book/series has a chance to find its audience.

How to write a reversion request

This is another instance when I googled what to say when asking for reversion. From my research and what I wrote to my publisher, the more succinct the letter is, the better for everyone. This isn't the time to write a manifesto.

My template is a jumping off point, and not the only way you can ask, but it worked for me.

Also, I had asked for reversion for a book within the rights reversion period, and one that was not fulfilled, which is an important distinction and why I've offered two examples on the next pages.

An editable version of these letters is available at katlynduncan.com/reversionletter.

Sample letter: If reversion specifications have been met.

[Date]

Dear [Contact],

I am writing to request that per [Publishing contract Identifier] the rights for [Title] revert to me, the author.

[This is where you state your terms according to the contract and how they have been fulfilled, i.e. It has been seven years since publication and the book is selling under 250 units over the last quarter...]

I request a written confirmation of rights reversion for my records. You can [email/mail to me at XXX]

[Complimentary close]
   [Your Name]

Sample letter: If reversion specifications have not been met.

[Date]

Dear [Contact],

I am writing to request that [Title] in [Publishing contract Identifier] revert to me, the author.

[This is where you explain why the publisher should revert the rights, whether you are looking for all of them or a specific sub-right. You may need evidence of sales, or lack of publisher exercising those rights, etc. The more you evidence you show, the better.]

I request a written confirmation of rights reversion for my records. You can [email/mail to me at XXX]

[Complimentary close]
    [Your Name]

Success Story: Kristine Asselin

Kristine Asselin is a hybrid author of both fiction and nonfiction for children and teens. She is the author of over fifteen books and going strong. You can find about more at kristineasselin.com.

KATLYN: What type of publisher did you have your books reverted from?

KRISTINE: A digital-first imprint.

KATLYN: What was the process of rights reversion like for you?

KRISTINE: The imprint for my first YA novel ('Any Way You Slice It') was Bloomsbury Spark. It came out in the spring of 2015. I don't think they ever got the readership that they had expected. I can't speak for others in the imprint, but my sales were pretty low. Two years after first publication, I heard through the grapevine that another author had requested and received their rights back. I asked my agent to look into it, and that was it. They reverted all rights and took the book off all platforms.

KATLYN: How did you get your rights back?

KRISTINE: My agent at the time did the legwork. As far as I can tell, it was an easy request. The imprint was no longer acquiring new work, and my editor had already left. It took less than six weeks to get permission.

KATLYN: After reversion, what plan did you have for this book?

KRISTINE: I wasn't able to get the cover without paying, so I left the original cover with the imprint. I worked with a small indie press editor and graphic designer (shout out to Kate Conway at Wicked Whale Press) to create new cover art and design the interior layout. I did a few minor edits, but largely kept the book the same. I'd never had a physical copy of 'Any Way You Slice It', so it was a dream come true to actually hold it in my hands when it finally published.

I did a full re-release/launch of the book in January 2018 and was so happy to be able to do that.

. . .

KATLYN: What was the republishing process like? Did you use a pen name? Did you go through KDP Select or wide (all platforms)?

KRISTINE: I republished with a small indie press called Wicked Whale Press. The book is available widely on all platforms and I do not use a pen name.

KATLYN: What monetary expenses did you expect? Were there any surprises?

KRISTINE: I paid my editor/designer for the formatting and cover design—she includes my books on her webpage (I published another YA with her in February 2019).

KATLYN: What is the best thing about having your rights reverted to you on this book?

KRISTINE: Being able to hold the book in my hand. I had a great experience with Bloomsbury and my editor there, but I don't think the imprint did what they had hoped it would do. I loved being able to take it back and do the sort of launch that felt right to me.

KATLYN: Any advice for authors who are going through rights reversion?

·   ·   ·

KRISTINE: I would say it doesn't hurt to ask, even if you think you're still under contract.

What if your publisher doesn't grant reversion of rights?

We can't discuss all the ways that you revert without talking about what happens when your letter goes unanswered, or the publisher wants to re-market the book.

This isn't necessarily a failure, because if the publisher believes in your book enough that they want to work to sell more, then that's great. But that is also the risk when signing a contract, which is why it's so important to make sure you are 100% aware of this before signing.

Unanswered request

If your publisher doesn't answer your formal request, this may need to escalate to someone else in the publishing house/imprint, your agent, or a lawyer. Especially if the rights reversion period is over and fulfilled, you should fight for your book. With a lawyer, you may incur initial costs, but with the rights given back to you, you have the opportunity to make all that back and then some.

The publisher wants to remarket your book

In my research, there have been successes and "failures". I put failures in quotation marks because when you request a book rights to be reverted to you, in contracts that I have seen (and heard of authors requests) there is a Reprint Demand which allows the publisher to in essence make the book "in print" once more. I've seen instances of publishers re-covering books, changing book blurbs, and/or adding extra marketing to a book to keep out of the danger zone of reversion.

You're too successful!

Another way that you wouldn't have the opportunity for reversion is that you are a successfully selling author.

This could come in two ways:

1. Your book is selling well. Most of us are in this business to sell books, and if you're doing that, then congratulations!

2. Another one of your books is selling well, and since front-list sells back-list, you may have to ride it out for longer than you expected. If you are determined to get your rights back, then you either have to wait it out or refer to Sample Letter 2 and see if you can get any sub-rights back.

Struggle Story: Terri Nixon

Terri Nixon is an author of historical fiction, family sagas, and mythic fiction. Her alter-ego, R.D. Nixon is the side of her that argues a lot and writes crime/thrillers. You can find her at terrinixon.com.

I wanted to thank Terri for exposing what her struggles have been like with asking for reversion after the clause has expired. This process can be frustrating, but if you are in this situation, you're not alone!

Take it away, Terri.

———

I originally asked for the rights back, for the two books I have with this publisher, before the 7-year time period specified in my contract. Putting aside the individual difficulties on release day, including one of them not being available all day, sales were unbelievably slow, despite really positive reviews. Repeated requests for price drops or promotions (or even a tweet or two!) came to nothing. The first book was published in 2014, the second one around a year later.

I was personally approached by Magna (Ulverscroft) for large print and audio rights, in early July 2016, and by October we were still trying to get a response from the publisher. We chased and chased, and were fobbed off at every turn with out of office messages, or "explanations" that the parent company was in Canada (yes, in this digital age!) and then claiming everyone was away at the various book fairs. I had to contact Magna again myself, to see if they were still interested – thank goodness, they were extremely patient.

At this point, my then-agent and I were just beginning to discuss the idea of the rights reversion, as it was clear the publisher had absolutely no intention of engaging with me over these titles – even when it would have been to their financial benefit. Luckily, they did contact Magna, eventually, and the sale of subsidiary rights went through in June 2017, almost a year after the initial offer. Direct quote from my agent:

"This one now goes down in history as the most ridiculous amount of chasing required ever!"

We even had contact from the head of the publishing house, accepting that this was an extremely poor performance on their part, and promising increased promotion for my books by way of recompense.

Nothing happened.

My agent initially wrote to the publisher to let them know we were asking for the reversion of rights, on November 23, 2017. She stressed to me that this was only a request, as the publisher was not obliged to return them at this stage. Rather than grant this request, they promised to *review the metadata, update the covers, and deliver a big push promotions-wise.* I agreed, and awaited the promised promotions and shareables. And waited a bit longer.

In May 2018 they made the covers a bit brighter and changed the titles. That was it. I then felt I had to shut up about it, because I'd agreed to their proposals and they'd fulfilled them.

The formal letter eventually went out from my agent to the publisher on October, 3 2019. There was no reason given, it was just a two-line email to say it was a formal request for the reversion of rights to the two titles. This was apparently passed on within the team, as my contact within the imprint was leaving. I heard nothing back.

My agent and I parted company in early 2020, since then I've been patiently waiting for the first of the books in question to reach the 7-year threshold. I wrote to the publisher myself, on February, 1 2021:

*This year sees seven years from the publication of my first book with you, and as you will see, sales have been poor from the outset. I have done my best to promote these books, in the face of complete indifference and half-hearted attempt at boosting their image, which was not backed up by any of the promised promotion. You have ruled out any hope of paperback, even POD [*Print on Demand*], for these titles, and they remain the only two of my books not available in this format.*

As noted below, I am no longer represented by (--), but I'm writing to you now to once again request the reversion of my rights to the two novels in this series published by you.

I would appreciate it if you contacted me directly, and without too long a delay, as this has now been going on for some years.

They asked me to hold on for a couple of months while they considered the best plan of action, and since I had that long left on my contract, I agreed. In early May this year [2021] I sent them an image of my royalty statement, stamped "too small to pay." This was for two books, over three months. I added the following:

...I have put in every bit as much hard work as I do for my other publishers, and was led to expect some degree of support, especially from a high-profile publisher such as yourselves. I'm not being difficult, and I've never had to do this before, but this has been the heart-breaking final straw.

I hope you will have something helpful for me, or will now agree to discuss the reversion of my rights so that I can make a clean break and move on.

During the course of the ensuing conversation, I mentioned that one of the main reasons for requesting my rights back was the paperback issue. People ask about them all the time, and I want to be able to offer this format–and also to return to their original titles; changing the names on the e-books had no effect, and merely caused confusion with the large print and audio titles, which hadn't changed.

The current position, as of May 18, 2021: I have had a promise, exactly three years on from the first, almost identical, one: they will: *review the metadata, update the blurbs, and deliver a big push promotions-wise...* hmm!

They also want to unlink these two books from the first in the series, which is with a different publisher. They have now said they'll take the books to a meeting with the sales director, and "*will definitely put your books on their radar and keep my eye out for any other opportunities in the meantime.*" They have said they need a retailer opportunity from somewhere like The Works, and as this chain has always been keen to buy decent quantities of my paperbacks in the past, I'm hoping they might pick these up too. If not, I'm still going to push to get my rights back.

For anyone else in the same, or similar, situation, I

would say that if you feel your publisher is under-performing, you have the right to call them to account; a contract works both ways, and it's in their interests, after all. They need to look beyond the shiny debuts, and the *next big things*, and acknowledge people like us, who are still out there, working like mad to produce books for them to sell.

What to do while waiting for rights reversion

Like most processes in publishing, this could take a while. On their end, they have to review the contract, and hold meetings before either accepting the reversion or rejecting it.

In the meantime, other than refreshing your email for their response, there are steps to prepare for their agreement.

As most books are on Amazon, currently the largest online book retailer, you want to copy/screenshot/print:

- The blurb/summary of your book
- Product details
- ASIN: this is Amazon's identifying number that will help link reviews from the previous version, if you choose to republish the book. More on that soon.
- ISBN (all formats)
- The original publication date
- Print length

- Trim size (if available in print, get these sizes for paperback, hardback, large print, etc.)
- Categories for all the formats you have available
- All of your reviews. I will explain why shortly. If you are an author who doesn't read reviews, have a friend collect them for you. If you are wide (your book is available on all platforms) grab the reviews from all the retailers and Goodreads.

Once your publisher takes these books down, you will no longer have access to these details. I suppose you could ask for them, but after you break up with someone, there's a bit of awkwardness left over, which is usually better left alone.

What happens after reversion?

Take a moment to celebrate. The path for your book has opened up wider than ever and you are ready to start on the next step of your journey.

Now what?

We're going to get to that soon, but first, a few housekeeping items.

The first is do not...

I repeat

Do not try to get this book published with another publisher.

9.99 times out of ten it's not going to work.

Once there is a sales record, copyright, any publication of a book with another publisher, no one wants to see it.

Of course, I'm sure there are one or two books in history that have done this, but I haven't heard of them, and in this business, you can't come in expecting to be the unicorn. Because even the unicorns don't expect that sprinkle dust until it magically grows their bank account.

The reason you asked for your rights to be reverted

was because of some deep-rooted unhappiness with your publisher that perhaps you can't explain or maybe you can.

Think about the times you asked for a change in the cover, or possibly exercising sub-rights and you were denied or ignored. Remember that time where you didn't hear from your editor for three weeks on a simple question and had to chase someone else who had the control over your book.

I'm digging deep here and it's for a reason.

I've fallen for it too.

In the past, I metaphorically blindfolded myself while signing a contract because it was nice to feel wanted and validated. I even ignored the clauses of a contract that didn't seem quite right. But if a publisher wanted me, then they would take care of my book the way I would, right?

Not always.

That signature gives away most of the control you have over anything other than the actual words. Even those can be threatened by a "vision" that a publisher has for the book.

Are we going to fall back into old habits?

Now, I'm not saying that once you revert you can't take part in another publishing deal. But not for this book. Take this as an opportunity to start fresh.

The ability to ebb and flow with the publishing industry is to get your hands dirty with failing before you succeed, then failing a little more. Self-publishing may seem daunting and unattainable, but with the right amount of willpower and perseverance, that "full-time author" status will come eventually with a much bigger reward.

Publication Files

Throughout any publishing process, especially those with a publisher, keep all your drafts of the book.

This may seem obvious, but when you're faced with rights reversion and the prospect of creating the files for uploading onto book platforms, and you only have the first draft of your book in your possession or have to pay out a significant chunk of money for the production files, you're going to want to tear your hair out.

For me, as a digital-first published author, I'd see copyedits and then a final digital copy of my book (usually in .epub format). There were no proofreading or formatting drafts that were available to me.

A lot of authors post those pretty pass pages online where it's their final say in changing anything in the book. Guess where those copies go? Back to the publisher. At that point, maybe they have the digital files for the version before that, but not with those final tweaks. I suppose some authors could translate them into the last version of the book they have, but I've never heard of anyone doing that.

In the case of *The Life After* series, after reversion, I asked about purchasing the production files—as stated in my contract. They agreed with a price. That cost on its own was affordable for one book, but for the set? It was obscene! Also, the cost of the files was more than half of what I made on the third book in the series. At that point, I already had a plan of republishing these books, and I felt that my money was best spent elsewhere on the production of these books (i.e. edits and covers).

So, keep your drafts. Even better, if you can have access to author copies of the digital files you won't have to resort to a publisher squeezing as much dough stained with your blood, sweat, and tears out of the deal.

Outstanding Editions

Months after 'Soul Taken' was reverted to me, I spotted my book still available on Apple Books. After a brief email to my previous editor, it was taken down within a few days. Sometimes it takes a little while for the books to completely come down, so I would recommend setting a reminder on your calendar to check all book retailers for your reverted books a couple of months later, and follow up with your previous editor or your contact at the publisher to remove them as soon as they can.

Making decisions about the future of your book

You have the formal letter from your publisher that your rights have been reverted to you, and you've managed to either secure the production files or you cleverly have kept the most recent draft of the novel. Now, you have some decisions to consider.

Do nothing with your book

I'm going to start with the option that won't create any additional work for you, which will also never bring another penny into your pocket.

That's the option to do nothing.

There's no judgment here. You created a book and someone else published it. You had a good run, sold some books, and hopefully learned a lot about the publishing industry. Whether that book was your first or tenth, you will have grown from the process.

You might be at a tipping point where you're interested in heading in a different direction with your career by publishing in another genre or this book no longer fits into your plan.

That's okay.

You gained knowledge and experience. That's worth its weight in gold.

There are so many people who want to write books and talk about it for years and still don't have a book to show for it. You've accomplished something that they could not. Take pride in that. It's okay to take the lessons learned and apply them forward to future projects.

Minimal effort

Feeling confident in your work is an amazing thing. If you are happy with the book as is, and reverted to give the book a new life for new readers, then all you need to do is format the book, re-cover it (more on that in Part II), and upload to retailers.

It's worth noting, that if this book no longer fits your backlist, or you don't want to bother with republishing it, you could use it as a newsletter builder if it's in the genre that you're wanting to find readers for. It's already written, and edited, so why not use it to draw readers to your newsletter? Exclusive and complete works are one of the best ways to attract readers to your list.

Considerations for using the book as a free promotional tool/reader magnet include the cover and distribution.

As this book isn't going up for sale anywhere, it doesn't need to have the best cover in the world, but it should have one. As we are discussing minimal effort, to keep costs low you can go with a premade or DIY approach.

Premade covers from a cover designer are usually a cost-effective alternative. These are covers that are pre-created and the designer will make minor tweaks such as changing the title and author name to yours. Usually design elements remain as-is.

To create your own, you can use Photoshop, Canva, or whatever design platform you prefer. This is the only instance I would recommend creating a cover on your own (unless, of course, you are a cover designer), as you're not selling the book and that cover isn't the main marketing tool for your book.

How you want to distribute this book to your readers is entirely up to you. The options include sending the book directly to your readers or through a distributor.

If you wish to send the book directly, you can email or set up an automation with your newsletter platform to everyone who signs up to your list with the file of the book. A downfall, this might be time consuming for you to send and/or troubleshoot any issues the reader might have. My advice for this route is to create a template email that you can copy and paste to make this easier. Adding instructions for each of the major e-readers would be helpful as well.

To make things a little easier, there are several companies out there ranging in cost that will host your reader magnet on their website. All you have to do is email the link to the subscriber or generate an automation within your newsletter provider to download the book. Most of these services will handle the troubleshooting which will take less time away from you. These companies include Bookfunnel, Story Origin, and Prolific Works (formerly Instafreebie).

Success Story: Katie Carroll [Picture Book]

Katie Carroll is a hybrid children's book author. Her titles include an award-winning YA fantasy series, 'Elixir Bound', and 'Elixir Saved', a middle grade adventure story, 'Pirate Island', and a picture book, 'The Bedtime Knight', which she talks about her reversion process below. Check her out at katielcarroll.com.

KATLYN: What type of publisher did you have your books reverted from?

KATIE: A digital-only imprint.

KATLYN: What was the process of rights reversion like for you?

. . .

KATIE: My publisher was bought by a bigger publisher, so there was a new contract being offered. I attempted to negotiate terms that weren't to my satisfaction, but the new publisher wouldn't accept any of the changes in my counteroffer. I declined to sign the new contract and my rights were reverted back to me. This was for a picture book where I was the author only, so all of this was only in regard to the text, not the illustrations.

KATLYN: How did you get your rights back?

KATIE: There was some paperwork I had to fill out to wrap up final payments. The new agreement had a date that I had to sign by, so when I didn't sign by that date, the rights were reverted back to me. All my communications went through one person at the new publisher, who would forward along information to pertinent people at the company and then would directly email me with any follow up. I did have to do some follow up as my book preview ended up on their website/app after the rights were mine.

KATLYN: After reversion, what plan did you have for this book?

KATIE: I did a light revision on the text of this book and sent it out to a few publishers that were open to submissions and didn't get any offers. Then I set the book aside for a while, not sure what I wanted to do with it. I would occasionally get inquiries from readers asking if that book would be available again. Eventually I contacted the original illustrator and asked if she would be interested in selling me the rights to self-publish the book. We came to terms and she wrote up a contract, so I purchased the rights to the original illustrations to publish it.

KATLYN: What was the republishing process like? Did you use a pen name? Did you go through KDP Select or wide (all platforms)?

KATIE: I did not use a pen name, in part because the cover art already had my name on it. The process was very involved with the design of this book because I had to adjust the illustrations myself. The original digital book was text on left side and illustration on the right. I wanted to do a print version with the common 32-page layout, and this design didn't work well for that. When I did finally republish it, I went wide.

KATLYN: What monetary expenses did you expect? Were there any surprises?

KATIE: There weren't any monetary expenses that surprised me as this was the fourth book I self-published. It was all the design issues that cost me time with this book.

· · ·

KATLYN: What is the best thing about having your rights reverted to you on this book?

KATIE: I was always so sad about not having this book available to readers and wondered if I should have just taken the contract when the publisher got bought out. But now that it's out and in print for the first time, I'm really happy that I did it on my own terms.

KATLYN: Any advice for authors who are going through rights reversion?

KATIE: Don't be afraid to go with your gut feeling, even if that means walking away from immediate money or opportunities. If you don't feel good (not just cold-feet nerves) about terms, it's worth it to negotiate or to walk away. There will be other opportunities for a book you believe in... even if you have to make your own!

Deciding to re-publish

You came to this section because you want this book to continue to work for you. There are several more questions to answer before deciding on the path you want for your reverted book.

Let's reread that last part: deciding on the path *you* want for your reverted book.

Feels good, right? That control gets addictive, so be aware that once you go down the self-publishing route, you may never go back.

Right now, you have the production files from your previous publisher, or the most edited draft that you have in your possession.

Read the book

Download it to your e-reader of choice or print it out and read it.

It may be years since you read the book, or you may be the type to reread your work every year on the anniversary of its publication date. No matter where you fall, this read-through is going to be different.

Before flipping to that first page, put that publisher hat on. Think of the audience for your book. You may already have a clear idea of who your ideal reader is, but if not, read with them in mind. With all aspects of book production and marketing, keep this reader front and center.

Now it's time to don your editorial glasses. For this first read-through, read the book from cover to cover without stopping to take notes (if you want to highlight your initial thoughts, I'm not over your shoulder watching you) but your goal is to note the condition of this book. Also, think about your vision for the story.

Remember that character you loved that your editor made you cut? Maybe they come back. Or did a plot hole haunt you? Fill that in. Did a pop culture reference not age gracefully? Take it out or adjust to fit current times. Now that you have all the possibilities in the world with this book, it's time to fix it!

After you read the book, jot down all your ideas. I suggest keeping a running list in a notebook, on your computer, or phone, or however you would keep notes during your routine editing process.

Read the reviews

Remember when I mentioned to keep those reviews from retailer websites? Now, it's time to pull them out.

If you haven't, there are other places where reviews don't disappear when the book is taken down that are ripe for pulling this feedback.

- Goodreads - I caution that this is a social

platform for readers to express the extremes of their feelings about books, both positive and negative. Tread lightly.

- Blog Tour - Many launch strategies for books involve a virtual tour element. Most of the time the host will have a list of all the links on their website. Search for the participant links and pull those reviews.
- Trade reviews - If you are lucky enough to get trade reviews from the bigger publishing platforms, grab those too.
- Google - Outside of launch tours, readers have their own websites where they like to talk about books. Google your name plus the book title (i.e. "Katlyn Duncan" "Soul Taken") to find reviews from readers who took the time to read your book and talk about it on their website.
- Social platforms - easiest to search, but like Goodreads, tread lightly.
- Instagram, YouTube, and TikTok - At the time of this writing, these are the platforms where a lot of readers hang out. The Bookstagram, BookTube, and BookTok communities are large and love to show off the books they love (and the ones they don't). Search for your name and title in hashtags. Take notes on the positives and negatives about the book.

As an aside, I understand that reading reviews is hard for a lot of authors. To be honest, I don't read any of mine anymore. After 'Soul Possessed' came out, I went through a dark time after I read lower starred reviews.

Sometimes it would send me into a paralyzing phase where I couldn't even write. I understand critical reviews are a rite of passage, but there is also a real person attached to the author name.

To circumvent this, I found that having someone else sift through these reviews for me was what I needed to take advantage of mining feedback for my books. A writer friend and I look at each other's reviews and find those lovely shareable quotes for us to put on social media, and also search for any consistent critical feedback from readers. There is no personal attachment when I'm reading her reviews or vice versa, which makes it a little easier to handle when the criticism inevitably comes.

Read between the lines

Right now, you have all the reviews, or your friend has curated them for you. Rank the reviews by best to worst (or the opposite if you are feeling particularly strong that day) and look for the following:

5-star reviews

These are where true fans are made (or these are your most supportive family and friends). These readers enjoyed the experience of reading your book so much that they want to shout it from the rooftops. This is where you can pull quotes for shareable images, but remember, you still have your publisher hat on.

Did these readers love the characters? The plot? The relationships? The escapism? Do you feel the same rush of excitement after reading the book for these aspects?

These reviews are also mood boosters. When I'm feeling somewhat low in the drafting or editing trenches, I'll pull these up and know that I am not a complete fraud.

4 and 3-star reviews

The real goods are in these reviews, and you will spend much of your time with these because they will have that critical feedback that you can use to improve your book. I lump these together because in a four star-review you may be able to parse together why they didn't want to give you that last glowing star. These readers will tell you what didn't work for them and sometimes at great length.

For example, if you wrote a romance novel and the reader was unhappy that the couple ended up together, this might not be the book for them as they don't appreciate genre standards.

But if your romance reader is upset that you broke their trust by not following through with a specific trope that you set up earlier in the book, or she felt the ending was rushed, those are important editorial notes and potential fixes.

2 and 1-star reviews

I don't find these reviews particularly helpful since most of the time they are mean, and even more so, these readers are usually not your audience. Information you can find from these readers is that if the book has more of these reviews than the higher star ratings, then there may be something inherently wrong with the book. Whether that's with the story, grammar issues, or issues with how the publisher marketed it (i.e. a story marketed as steampunk when its core lies with dystopian).

———

Once you have gathered the feedback, skim through it with the distance you should have as a publisher. This isn't the time to wallow in people not liking your book. You took back this book for a reason, you want to do something with your second chance, so why not make it the best book you can?

From this feedback, decide what aspects you want to fix. When that is done, you have an editing plan.

Success Story: Madeline Dyer

Madeline Dyer is an award-winning young adult author of dark and twisty books. Her books include the *Untamed* series, the *Dangerous Ones* series, and 'Captive: A Poetry Collection on OCD, Psychosis, and Brain Inflammation'.

You can find her at madelinedyer.co.uk.

KATLYN: What type of publisher did you have your books reverted from?

MADELINE: An independent/small press.

KATLYN: What was the process of rights reversion like for you?

. . .

MADELINE: The publisher closed, but all the authors ended up having to individually request that our rights were reverted.

KATLYN: How did you get your rights back?

MADELINE: I mailed a formal letter to the publisher—as stated should be done in the contract—and also an email. It was quite a few years ago, and I believe it was the email that they replied to a few days later, confirming rights had reverted to me. A year later, the letter I'd mailed was returned to me unopened.

It had become a very stressful process, because prior to the publisher announcing they were closing, they'd stopped paying royalties (which are still outstanding, years later), so several of us authors were already worried and stressed by this. One of the other authors had a legal background and she helped me pen my letter requesting the rights reversion.

However, even after my rights had reverted, they were still selling new print-on-demand copies of my books for quite a while, which was the more stressful part as they were still making money from my work.

I was also one of the lucky authors as I heard from others that they'd had no reply to their requests for rights reversions.

KATLYN: After reversion, what plan did you have for this book?

.   .   .

MADELINE: This concerned the first two books in my *Untamed* series, and I was already about half done with drafting the third book in the series and had a loyal fanbase. I knew I wanted to keep telling this story, so I sought advice and help from indie writers and re-released books one and two myself. I only did a very light extra edit on book two (as I'd not been happy with the editing services provided by the publisher on that book), but essentially the story and text stayed largely the same. It was important to me not to add any new details to the story that my existing readers would miss out on—so I had to make sure that book three worked based on the first editions of books one and two.

KATLYN: What was the republishing process like? Did you use a pen name? Did you go through KDP Select or wide (all platforms)?

MADELINE: I launched the books wide, across all major e-book and paperback retailers.

KATLYN: What monetary expenses did you expect? Were there any surprises?

MADELINE: I covered the costs of the new cover design and interior design, as well as buying the ISBNs and registering them to my own imprint, Ineja Press. I invested a bit in marketing too, and really hyped up the relaunch. I was lucky that I was able to hire an editor for book three who just so happened to have already read book one in the series when it was first published by the publisher.

KATLYN: What is the best thing about having your rights reverted to you on this book?

MADELINE: The creative control! I love having input in the cover design, but also on an editorial level too. I'd had a few issues with the editing of book two in particular—I had been told I had to change a character's name because the spelling meant it was apparently too unfamiliar and unpronounceable (in the editor's opinion). Although that character was renamed in book two, I was then able to use that original name for another character in book four. This was really important to me, as I didn't want to have all the characters' names following Western conventions.

I was also able to write exactly what I wanted to for the subsequent books—it was a lot more freeing.

KATLYN: Any advice for authors who are going through rights reversion?

MADELINE: Definitely check your contracts and know exactly how you need to request rights reversion—and also to know what exactly the publisher can claim ownership to. There was one point where the owners of my former publisher were claiming that they owned the edited versions of our books and if we wanted to republish them we'd have to go back to the first draft we sent them and edit it afresh from there, meaning all the developmental, line, and copyedits would have to be redone so we had sufficiently different stories. This seemed ridiculous, as it would've meant huge changes to the plot to make it 'different enough' and I was very stressed by this at first, as I had readers already waiting for the third book. I couldn't rewrite books one and two, taking them in a whole new direction—and I didn't want to. One of the publisher's editors later confirmed that this information the owners had been giving us was incorrect and that we could use the final versions of our books, after all. All the publisher could claim ownership of were the covers and interior formatting—though this only applied to some books, as it turned out there were issues over the designers not being paid too, just like the authors and editors.

Completing a light edit

A light edit may involve as little as fixing a few typos, bringing the dialogue and/or prose to the writing level you're at today, while preserving most of the story.

In the instance of 'Soul Taken', the first book in *The Life After* series, this book is my baby. I will forever love the story. After reversion, I didn't want to change much about it, but I worked on deepening descriptions, making world-building clarifications, and tweaking dialogue to make my characters more rich.

Since it had been seven years from publication, I worked with my editor on a developmental edit (we treated this like critique partner feedback) and a line edit. There wasn't much in terms of development, but it really focused on clarifying the story for the reader and picking out world-building inconsistencies and issues.

After her, I worked through another edit for myself, and then did an in-depth grammar check with ProWritingAid. This picked up even more style and grammar issues.

Then, I sent it to a proofreader to highlight the last of the issues before calling it a final draft.

Success Story: Katie Carroll [Young Adult Novel]

Katie Carroll has another reversion experience that we wanted to share, separate from her picture book.

KATLYN: What type of publisher did you have your books reverted from?

KATIE: A digital-first imprint.

KATLYN: What was the process of rights reversion like for you?

KATIE: My original contract was for a specific period and that amount of time had passed for the published book when I was figuring out what to do with a second unpublished manuscript in the series. The contract had a right of first refusal for sequels, so I would have had to submit first to the publisher of the first book unless I terminated the contract. I decided to move in a different direction with the series and asked for my rights back for the published book with the intent of self-publishing both books.

KATLYN: How did you get your rights back?

KATIE: In order to get my rights back, I simply wrote an email to the owner of the publishing company, who was my contact for all contract and royalty questions or issues. She agreed to grant all rights back to me (they had e-book and print rights) and emailed me a letter saying I had my rights back. She also mentioned that if a future publisher needed confirmation that the company had reverted the rights, they could email her.

KATLYN: After reversion, what plan did you have for this book?

KATIE: My plan was to repackage and publish the book myself. I was happy with the content of the book and previous edits, so I did a light edit for a few minor content issues and to clean up any lingering typos/copyedits.

KATLYN: What was the republishing process like? Did you use a pen name? Did you go through KDP Select or wide (all platforms)?

. . .

KATIE: I did not use a pen name when I republished the book myself. I had already self-published another novel under my name, so I was comfortable staying with it. I went wide with distribution for e-book and paperback, which were both released at the same time. I wasn't able to publish under the same cover, but that was okay because I wanted a new cover to rebrand. I hired an illustrator I had worked with before to do a new cover for the first book and also a cover for the second book in the series when it was ready.

KATLYN: What monetary expenses did you expect? Were there any surprises?

KATIE: I expected to put most of my republishing budget into the cover. I had already self-published a book before this, so there weren't any unexpected expenses.

KATLYN: What is the best thing about having your rights reverted to you on this book?

KATIE: Having already self-published a book before this one, I really knew I would like the control I would have over the process. Being able to control the distribution channels and seeing which ones sold the most copies and getting paid directly from them was empowering. I also wanted to have control over the series itself, which was important to me with the second book in the series (and any future books I decided to write from that world).

KATLYN: Any advice for authors who are going through rights reversion?

KATIE: Be patient with yourself. Take the opportunity to learn what interests you, but also don't be afraid to hire out for the parts that you have no interest in learning about. There are so many decisions that go into self-publishing a book that it's easy to get overwhelmed, so take it one thing at a time. Trust your gut on the decisions you make, too.

Completing a heavy edit

If you're the author who cringes when people say they've picked up your book because you wrote it "x" amount of years ago, and you know you are so much better now. Or your editor suggested an idea that you agreed with at the time, but maybe reviewers noted how it didn't work for the story.

This is where all the tweaks lie, from altering characters and/or plot to a point where a reader who has experienced the story before would still recognize it but know that it's not quite the same. Which hopefully means you've improved it!

With 'Soul Possessed', the second book in *The Life After* series, I needed to work a little harder. At the end of 'Soul Taken', I changed a line that altered the start of 'Soul Possessed'. I also wanted to make 'Soul Possessed' stronger, so I added more depth to my side characters.

This involved a reworking of the outline before a rewrite. It was easier for me to get through the story without piecing together paragraphs from the original book, as most of the characters, interactions, settings, world-building, and the bigger mystery of the story stayed the same.

Success Story: Keri Stevens

Keri Stevens writes small-town paranormal romances. Her debut, 'Romancing the Stone Witch', won two international awards for best first book and for paranormal romance. You can find her at keristevens.com.

KATLYN: What type of publisher did you have your books reverted from?

KERI: A traditional (Big 4) publisher.

KATLYN: What was the process of rights reversion like for you?

KERI: The terms expired—I sold under one hundred copies for a certain period of time.

. . .

KATLYN: How did you get your rights back?

KERI: My process with Harlequin/HarperCollins was super-simple: After re-reading my contract, I determined that with my low recent sales on the book I could request rights back. HQN [Harlequin] has an author portal where I found instructions to make my request. I emailed my agent on the book to notify her I'd be requesting the rights back in order to self-publish. I then emailed the contact at HQN with my contract number and a very brief email saying, "Please give me my rights back," and copied my agent.

These were very short, matter-of-fact emails: "I am requesting my rights back. Please let me know the next steps. Thank you." There was and is no need to go into explanations about why I made the choice or apologies for leaving or any feelings I had.

The agent (who has always been great) basically thanked me for letting her know and wished me luck. HQN notified me the review process would take about 90 days—and indeed, it did. In May 2021, I got an email telling me my rights on the book reverted to me and that I no longer have the right to promote or use the cover materials.

I asked my assistant to take down any references to the book online, as well as cover imagery on sites/social media I control. As of today, the book is gone from all retailers, except for Audible*. Publishers have licensing agreements with companies like Audible. When I reread my reversion letter, I noted the licensing clause and emailed my contact person at HQN.

. . .

* [addendum from Keri] Because contract timelines with Audible differed from those with the e-book, it took HQN an additional quarter to fully complete my reversion of rights. They gave me a date for the end of that contract and, indeed, the book was down the day after. I adjusted my timeline for republishing the book only slightly. The revised and re-titled version of the book with a fresh ISBN will go up as indie.

KATLYN: After reversion, what plan did you have for this book?

KERI: I'm doing moderate edits right now (adding a few new scenes, deleting some irrelevant side characters, adding material to better fit it into the building series). This will be a reader magnet into the series.

KATLYN: What was the republishing process like? Did you use a pen name? Did you go through KDP Select or wide (all platforms)?

KERI: The plan is to place the series in KU initially, then eventually publish wide.

KATLYN: What monetary expenses did you expect? Were there any surprises?

· · ·

KERI: I've not been surprised (so far) by expenses: I knew I'd rely heavily on my assistant for research into current fantasy romance trends and expectations. I knew I'd buy a new cover. I knew I'd pay for some editing. I haven't yet decided how to handle ads but will get into that as I finish the next two books in preparation for a rapid release.

KATLYN: What is the best thing about having your rights reverted to you on this book?

KERI: Control. Control over the publishing timeline. Control over promotion. Control over marketing. Control over sales outlets. The flip-side, of course, is that what happens from now on is my responsibility. The buck stops here—but then I get to put it in the bank.

KATLYN: Any advice for authors who are going through rights reversion?

KERI: I flip-flopped heavily between editing this book and drafting its sequel, which wasted a lot of time.

On one hand, the reverted book wasn't "mine" until last week, so time spent on it (and money spent on its cover) might have been wasted if HQN had said "no." This was a very low risk because that book had very low sales.

On the other hand, book two in the series is mine, guaranteed, so there was no risk to working on that.

If I had to do over again, I would have just made one decision and stuck with it. Both choices are valid, but I could have saved myself some angst.

Complete rewrite

This is the polar opposite from doing nothing and putting the book in the drawer forever. This is as close as you can get to throwing all the words away, but I'm sure you'll keep some of the "a's" "and's" and "the's".

That original seed of the story remains, but it is a stark contrast from the original. This is where that reader who bought the book seven years ago picks it up again and maybe recognizes the character names, if you left those alone, but the story is entirely new for them.

It's also the most expensive option when it comes to money and time. This may seem overwhelming, but you have to really love this book and want to see it polished and available once more to the reading world. If you've made proper notes during your read-through, hopefully you are excited to implement them and shine up the story to its best potential.

As of the writing of this book, I haven't started working on the production of 'Soul Betrayed', the third book in *The Life After* series yet, but I have a plan. This book needs an overhaul. When I re-read it, there were so many instances of me struggling to wrap up storylines that it was rushed, and to be honest, I only want to keep the beginning and ending.

This is going to involve a new outline, draft, editing, the works.

Rights Reversion – Review And Actionable Steps

Actionable steps for The Contracted Author

- If you want to republish, keep an eye on those reversion terms. Mark them in your calendar or set a reminder on your phone for when they expire.
- Prepare your reversion letter ahead of time to get ready for the day they revert to you.
- Track sales from royalty reports to build your case for reversion.
- Note the contact at the publisher to send the reversion letter.
- If you are interested in signing another contract with a publisher, pay close attention to the reversion clause. Work with your agent or lawyer to get the terms to where you need them to be.
- Ensure that you keep and file all the versions of your book as you go through edits.

After Reversion

- Inquire with the publisher about cost of production files.
- Gather the books' production files.
- Decide if/how you want to republish the book.

If republishing,

- Read the book as a publisher.
- Read the reviews
- Create an editing plan.
- Decide which type of edit(s) you need for the book.

Actionable steps for The Hopeful Contracted Author

- Acquire a professional to review the contract before signing.
- If you sign away your rights, save every single iteration of your book.

Actionable steps for The On-The-Fence Author

- Connect with other authors who are with publishers and ask about royalty rates, option clauses, and reversion clauses. Inquire about how much control they have over their books. Question yourself about what rights you want to have for your book, and hopefully that will help you decide.

Part II: The Path to Self-Publishing

The path to self-publishing

With self-publishing, there are a lot of choices to make since there is no longer someone else to make them for you. Throughout this time, I reached out to my amazing group of writer friends who've been there to help me, along with researching every facet of independent publishing.

The biggest choices for this process involve money, and the ranges vary depending on who you hire and for what. I'm going to start with covers and editing as those will most likely be the largest part of your budget. Covers sell books and once you get the reader, the polished interior will keep them hooked and hopefully create a life-long fan.

Cover design

With all the publishing options discussed, most of the time, you will have to get a new cover. Bigger publishers have internal art departments who create covers for their authors, which gives them ownership over the artwork. Even if the cover was outsourced by the publisher, licensing of images and/or illustrations may get a little tricky and usually aren't offered to the reverted author.

But there's no harm in asking.

If you get the cover back, fantastic! Get the original files (if possible) so you can tweak if you ever need to. These files may come at a price, so prepare yourself for that.

If you don't like the cover your publisher chose, or they refused to give you the rights to it, you will need a new one. Which means you will have to purchase a premade cover or have one custom designed for you.

Again, unless you are a cover designer, I highly recommend hiring out for this one. This is the best marketing tool you will ever have for your book, and just because your friend has a graphic design degree doesn't mean they will create one that will stop a reader from browsing the book store and make them to buy your book. Book covers are their own beast. It's not just about creating a pretty image, you want the cover to portray the feel of your book while reflecting the genre.

I didn't bother asking for the rights to the covers of *The Life After* series. At the point of reversion, the books had been out for over seven years, and while the cover art was stunning, they weren't in line with current young adult paranormal cover trends. Again, we're trying to go forward instead of back. Yet, the obvious disadvantage of this was paying a designer for three new covers up front in e-book and paperback format. Oof.

Also, if your plan is to exercise your sub-rights, with hardback, audio, and, if you have a series, a digital box set cover, these come with specifications and tweaks of the design that will cost extra.

Where to find designers

Book research

Find books in your genre on your bookshelves and/or your favorite online book retailer (Amazon, B&N, Kobo, Google Play, Apple Books), and check out the bestselling ones. Most books have their cover designer listed on the copyright page, which is usually included in the preview or sample of the book. Start making a list of the designers.

Author recommendations

I always do my own research, but often inquire with my writer friends, asking who they used for their books. The independent author community is largely made up of writers who want to help each other, and a personal recommendation can mean more. In this situation, you will get to know more about the designers working relationships right from the source.

Google search

Searching Google for "book cover design" will yield a lot of results, making it an option to quickly find designers.

Freelance websites

Websites like Fiverr and Upwork have freelancers ready to design your cover for you. Check their portfolios to make sure that their style is what you're looking for.

Curated services

BookBaby and Lulu offer design services in addition to many other self-publishing services.

What to look for and ask your designer

Your cover designer is in charge of creating your most valuable book marketing tool. Be sure you are a good fit from the start by researching and asking all the questions up front so there are no surprises.

Experience/Skill

Most designers will have a portfolio on their website of past projects. Look for their designs in your genre.

. . .

Price

Not all designers will have their pricing on their website. Inquire about this up front to make sure that they are in range of your budget. Also, designers may lower the cost if you want to do a series. Most of the time there are smaller changes between covers to keep them cohesive, so inquire if you are looking for a branded series and see if you can save some money there.

Timeline

Ask when their earliest availability is for your cover. If you need one in two months, and they're booked out for a year, this is an easy strike out on your list for that designer. Or if you really want to work with them, you may have to delay your release.

Initial options

Inquire about how many initial options you will have to choose from up front.

Revisions

How many revisions is the designer willing to do before the book cover is complete? This is important to know so you're aware of how to communicate with them when requesting changes.

Communication style

If you have questions, will they respond in a few

hours/days? Do they communicate via email, personal message, etc.?

Files

All designers are different, but at the very least should give you high-resolution images of the book cover formats that were agreed to (depending on if this is just e-book, or e-book and print). If you are interested in making your own adjustments to the cover at another point, ask if they offer the design files (i.e. Photoshop).

Referrals

If you were unable to get a referral up front, ask the designer if they could reach out to their previous clients to connect you with them to get the author-side of the experience. Ask the above questions of the author to get a better idea of working with this designer.

Types of covers

Premade Covers

If you have a tight budget, a lot of designers offer premade covers. This is where the cover is already made with the design elements (image, title/author/tagline font) and you have the designer change the title, author name, and/or tagline to yours. The amount of changes would depend on the designers specifications, which is usually listed on their website. I've seen these types of covers range from $50-200+.

Customized covers

These covers are designed specifically for your book. They will be the more expensive ones, ranging from $150-2000+ depending on what you're using for images (licensing of stock or custom images, custom images/illustrations may add to the cost).

The experience that I'm most familiar with (and most of my writer friends as well) is filling out a form or survey from the cover designer based on questions that try to depict the feel of your book, as most of the time the designers will not read it. This is similar to an art sheet that the editor at your publisher may give to an art department or a freelance designer. Questions can range from the broad strokes of the book (asking about genre and the summary of the book) to more specific (which covers in your genre do you like, why or why not, do you have a particular symbol or image you want to have on the cover, etc.)

As you no longer have an editor at a publishing house handling this for you, I highly recommend that you take the time to fill out this survey with as much detail as possible. This will help the designer create an option (or multiple options depending on the contract) that will sell your book with one look.

Hiring and working with editors

Until now, your publisher has most likely handled hiring and working with your editors. The editors you use now will depend on your budget and what type of edit you want to do.

Developmental Editors

Developmental editors work on the story as a whole, that big-picture work. They will look at the plot, characters, pacing, tense, and style of the story. Depending on the editors style they may give a report based on these elements and/or work within the document to note these suggestions.

In my experience, these types of edits would come from the editor who bought the book at the publisher. You may have gone through several rounds before moving onto the next stage of editing.

This editor will most likely not focus on the line-level edits, so give them the most polished version of your book so they can focus on what they're supposed to do. I expand this advice to every point in the process when you're working with editors.

If you are happy with the higher-level view of your book (as at this point your reverted book would have hopefully gone through edits at your publisher), you can call on writer friends (critique partners) to focus on these big-picture edits. I found that working with critique partners sped up the process with my editor as I had resolved a lot of the bigger issues prior to giving them the book.

Line Editors

Line editing focuses on what its name suggests, the line-level writing. This editor will look at sentence structure and language of the piece along with pacing and flow of the book.

Before working with a line editor, ensure that you are happy with the developmental type edits (whether you used an editor or critique partners). As they will mostly focus on line-level editing, it would be a waste of time and money for them to work on sentence structure and pacing if you have massive plot or character issues that need fixing.

Copy Editors

Typically, copyediting comes after line editing. This editor will focus on the mechanics of the line-level writing such as spelling, grammar, punctuation, and typos. This is the last line of defense before a proofread.

Proofreaders

Proofreading is the final pass of the editing process

before publication. Their job is to find typographical errors. They usually will not suggest story changes but will look for any text or formatting errors.

Editing Packages

Looking at all the types of editors might make you feel overwhelmed, or you may hear the draining of your bank account at the idea of hiring four different people to edit your project. While you shouldn't skip editing, many editors offer packages to authors, bundling the edits.

For instance, you might find an editor who will do both developmental and line edits, line edits and proof-reading, or copyedits and proofreading. This can be a time and cost saver for you.

If you are doing a heavy edit or complete rewrites, I would recommend at least two editors to help you. The more eyes on the manuscript the better.

How to choose an editor

After determining what type of edit(s) you want, how do you choose an editor?

Researching Editors

Ask your writer friends who they recommend as editors, or if you are a part of any online groups, ask within the group, or search posts for recommendations.

Also, if you are a member of any writer organiza-tions, usually you can search forums/groups, or there may be a list of recommended editors. For instance,

- SCBWI (Society for Children's Books Writers and Illustrators) has Member Forums where you can either post that you are looking for recommended editors or search through to find who others have recommended.
- The Alliance of Independent Authors has an opportunity to search through their Approved Services (editorial services included) and have member discounts as well.
- Google - Once again, Google comes in handy, but will yield a lot of results to sift through.

Choosing an Editor

Considerations for each type of editor:

- Experience: Does this editor have an advanced degree in a literature based creative art? Do they have certifications in editing? Or are they a part of a credited organization/association?
- Genre: Does this editor work in your genre? Specializing in your genre will only help your book as they would understand nuances of genre tropes, pacing, style, etc.
- Turnaround time: When can they get the book back to you with their edits? Does that fall within the timeline of your release schedule?
- Cost: This can vary widely, depending on the type of edit. But, because an editor might be

above or below the median, doesn't mean they aren't worth checking out.

According to a 2020 survey from the Editorial Freelancers Association, these are the media rates per word:

  Developmental editing: $.03–$.039/word
  Line editing: $.04–$.049/word
  Copyediting: $.02–$.029/word
  Proofreading: $.02–$.029/word

- Testimonials: Ask if you can contact a previous client of theirs. If they give you someone, take advantage and reach out to the author. Ask how they felt about working with said editor, what type of feedback they received, and if they were satisfied with the experience.
- Sample Edit: Does the editor do a sample edit? This is a good indicator of how they will work with you and what type of edits they supply. Usually these are offered free or at a cost for the editors time. Don't be deterred if they do charge. These are professionals and should get paid for their time. A lot of editors will remove that cost from the final payment if you decide to work with them. Don't be afraid to have several editors do this as you are looking for someone who shares your same vision for the book and will help bring it to the best level it can be before publication.

Working with an Editor

Now that you have your editor booked, how do you work with them? At this point, you may have only worked with an in-house editor at your publisher. This relationship (at least for me) is different when you are hiring someone on your own. As an author without an agent, I relied heavily on communication from my publisher's editor in most matters.

But a freelance editor will only handle what you pay for. If they offer more, that's great, but don't expect it. If you worked through the list in the previous section, you will have their timeline and communication style which will allow you and your editor to have as much of a harmonious relationship as possible.

Before sending your book

- Polish the book as much as you are able in any stage. If a book is riddled with grammar issues and typos, this may hinder an editor from diving deeper into your manuscript as they are correcting minor issues that could have easily been fixed with a grammar checker.
- As you are now your own publisher, deadlines are yours and yours alone. But working with any professional, you have to respect their time. It's best to schedule an editor months ahead if you can, as most will have other projects they are working on. So, stick to those deadlines. If you can't, inform them as soon as possible to the change. You're

building a team around you and it's common courtesy to respect their time as much as yours.

After getting your edits back

- Mindset: You have been through edits before, but you've hired this person to spot errors and now you are in charge of fixing them or not. Take any personal connections that you have with the book and put them aside and do the work that will improve your book.
- Communication: You don't want to waste your editor's time with questions about the book months after your edit was completed, at least read their notes or the manuscript and note any areas where you aren't clear about the edits and contact them right away for clarification.

Grammar Check

While human editors are always recommended for your book, there are some helpful plug-ins to popular writing programs (i.e. Scrivener and Word/Pages, etc.) to improve your writing.

I've used both ProWritingAid (PWA) and Grammarly as my last self-edit before sending to an editor. Grammar checkers like these are integral for catching more than grammar issues. They look at style as well, such as echoes in your writing, overused words, etc.

These checkers act more like a copyeditor and will be beneficial to teaching you about how you write and ways to improve. For instance, if you're seeing all passive voice throughout your manuscript, the constant reminder may help your drafting process become much cleaner.

For me, I have a nasty habit of repeating words within several sentences of each other. These checkers have allowed me to grow my vocabulary and improve the flow of my drafts.

ISBNs

ISBN stands for International Standard Book Number. These numbers identify a book-like product which is specific to format, edition, and publisher.

Your previous publisher would have handled this process in the initial printing or release of your book.

If you are republishing, you cannot use the original number as your ISBN because each publisher (including independent authors) are assigned these numbers. Which is also why I would never recommend purchasing an ISBN from someone other than the agency who distributes them. If you do, this company would "own" your book in a sense and it could get a little messy.

In the United States and its territories, the only company that sells ISBNs is Bowker (myidentifiers.com). In the U.K. they are sold through Nielsen (nielsenisbn-store.com). In Canada, you can get an ISBN for free. If you are outside of those territories, please research where you should find ISBNs based on your country. A simple Google search for "[your country]" "ISBN" should locate it quickly.

For the countries that sell ISBNs, you may have the option to buy one at a time or in bulk. Most of the time, the bulk costs are much lower than purchasing the single.

If you are republishing only one book, I would spring for a package that handles at least 5+ so you have the option of getting your book in as many formats as you want while being as cost effective as possible.

If you want to keep your upfront costs minimal, there are options for free identifying numbers on specific platforms:

- Amazon: KDP (Kindle Direct Publishing) provides a free identifier for e-books called an ASIN (Amazon Standard Identification Number), and they offer a free ISBN for print books.
- Barnes & Noble and Draft2Digital: Provides a free ISBN to publish your print book.
- IngramSpark: As of the writing of this book, IngramSpark offers free ISBNs for U.S. self-published authors.
- Kobo, Apple Books, and Google Play are e-book distributors only, and providing an ISBN is optional.

Pitfalls of free identifiers

- You can't take this number to another platform. For instance, you can't take the KDP free print ISBN and use that at Barnes and Noble or vice versa.
- Using a book platforms' number will list them

as the publisher of the book. While they don't
have a claim on your book, if you want to
appear like a professional and legitimate
publisher from the onset, I recommend using
your own.

- Once you use an ISBN (free or purchased),
  you cannot change it unless you create a new
  edition of the book.

For *The Life After* series, I purchased a bundle of 100-ISBNs. From the outset, I knew I wanted consistency on all the platforms, so I needed one ISBN per e-book (+3), one ISBN per paperback book (+3), and eventually I want to put the series in audiobook (+1-3 – I'm unsure if I want to publish the audiobooks in a single or set). Already that brings me close to the smallest package which is 10 ISBNs. As I'm planning to publish many more books, purchasing the next highest bundle was the obvious answer. The 100-ISBN package drives the price down to $5.75 per ISBN, versus the 10-ISBN package which is $29.50 per ISBN, and the 1-ISBN which is $125.*

*These prices are reflective of the time of writing.

Formatting your book

Have you ever read a book where the lines were broken up mid-sentence or the indents weren't consistent? It's uncomfortable and frustrating to read, isn't it?

That's formatting.

FYI: Some publishers carry a copyright for interior design so double check with them before republishing your production files.

Along with good editing, you want your book to look as professional and easy to read as possible. Typos and bad formatting will make a reader put down your book, no matter how fantastic the story or information is inside.

There are options for doing this yourself for free or some paid programs to help, along with hiring a formatter. This all depends on your budget and time. If you are willing to learn how to do it yourself, then you can update your books whenever you want and only pay with your time. Or, if you don't have the time, but have the money, hiring a professional formatter makes sense. A lot of them have design experience and can really enhance the look of your book.

Formatting Yourself

This is not a comprehensive list as new formatting tools are popping up each day, but at the time of this writing, these are the top contenders.

Free Options

- Google Docs / Pages [Mac] - You can format both e-book and print using these options.
- Draft2Digital - This is another free resource for e-book formatting. It's a fantastic tool for those with a tight budget, and you don't even need to upload your book using D2D to use it.
- Kindle Create - This free tool gives you the opportunity to create a formatted and publishable file for Kindle Direct Publishing for both e-book and print.

Paid Options

- Microsoft Word - With an Office subscription, or a one-time fee to download to your computer, you can format in Word. There are many templates and online tutorials to help figure out the nuances of the program. You can format both e-book and print using this option.

- Scrivener - Many writers use Scrivener as a drafting tool, but it can be useful as a formatting tool for e-books and print.
- Vellum - With Vellum, you can format both e-book and print books (depending on which plan you purchase). The downside is that it's only for Mac users or you can work with Mac In Cloud on a PC.
- Adobe InDesign - This robust tool will allow you to create a uniquely formatted book, depending on your experience with design. You can do both e-books and printed books.
- Atticus - At the time of this writing, Atticus is still in a beta testing phase, but it's a formatting tool available for Mac and PC-users for both paperback and e-book.

Hiring a formatter

- Research: Use the same steps and questions from how to choose an editor.
- Private freelancer - Like editorial services, you can work with a private freelancer, or many editorial freelancers offer formatting as a package within their services.
- Freelance - Freelance websites like Upwork and Fiverr have budget-friendly options for formatting novels.

Working with a formatter

Ask what their process is like with turnaround time and with revisions. The first turnaround time may be longer as they are formatting the book, than they are with revisions, but understand what both timing looks like regarding your production schedule. With revisions, have a clear idea on how many revisions the cost includes and then the cost of future revisions. For instance, if you want to add/change front or backmatter or fix typos.

Future relationship

As I mentioned, if you don't format your book yourself, then you will have to contact your formatter for any changes you want in the future. Save their most up-to-date contact information and understand the costs of revisions.

Copyright

While copyright pages are not linked to formatting specifically, if you choose to put a copyright page in the front or back matter of your book, you need information that you will either insert on your own or supply a formatter.

This page is optional, as your book is copyrighted the moment you write it, but as a self-published author, it's always a good idea to protect your rights when you can. It's one of the easiest pages to write in your book, and it defines you as the author, rights holder, and gives the proper information to booksellers, librarians, readers, and distributors.

Typically, the copyright page will appear after your title page in a print format. In e-books, I've seen them at the front or back. There are many templates online, or you can check out the books on your bookshelf or library for examples.

At the very least, the copyright page should include:

- The copyright notice
- The owner/publisher of the book
- Year of publication
- Book Edition*
- ISBN
- Credits to the book designer/editor/formatter (some cover designers require this in their terms)
- Disclaimer

---

*For the book edition, this is where reverted books can differ from first published ones. Depending on what type of edit you did, you may want to note that it's another edition, or when it was initially published.

In the United States, you can copyright your book online at Copyright.gov for peace of mind. There is a fee for this, but it will protect your book if anyone plagiarizes. If you are not in the U.S., check your government's laws about copyright.

The Path To Self-Publishing – Review And Actionable Steps

Edits

Decide which type of edit(s) you need for the book:

- Self-edit
- Critique partner feedback
- Developmental edit
- Line edit
- Copyedit
- Beta readers
- Proofread
- Cover design

Cover

- Decide on a Premade or Custom design for your cover
- Research cover designers
- Contact cover designer(s)
- Choose a cover designer

Editor(s)

- Research editors
- Contact editor(s)
- Sample edits
- Choose editor(s)

ISBN

- If using your own ISBN, research and purchase

Formatting

If formatting yourself,

- Choose a platform
- Learn the process

If using a professional formatter,

- Research formatters
- Contact formatter(s)
- Choose formatter
- Compile copyright information

Part III: Re-Publishing Your Book

Re-Publishing your book

Let's take a breath. You have successfully created a book-shaped thing without a publisher. How does that feel? Pretty good, right?

This is where more of the magic happens: Publishing your book so everyone can buy it for themselves!

Keeping Amazon reviews

To my knowledge, Amazon is the only platform that you can request to have your reviews transferred over from a previous edition.

Remember when I told you to keep all the information from the various vendors? Find that ASIN number that your publisher uploaded with. This ASIN is the key to restoring reviews for your book, both positive and negative.

If you've made significant changes to your book, or you had a lot of negative reviews, starting with a blank slate may be more work upfront but will only benefit you later.

Otherwise, having reviews will help boost your book as more "legit" shortly after publication.

To do this, once the book is uploaded and live, email the Amazon team through Author Central and request them to link the books and previous reviews.

Exclusivity versus Wide

Currently, there are two publishing paths that are discussed among the indie-author space when it comes to e-books, these are referred to as "exclusive" and "wide".

Exclusive refers to the KDP Select program on Amazon where you publish your e-book on their site exclusively for a minimum of 90 days (you can opt out at any time after each 90-day stint). There are benefits to this publishing path based on your vision for the book. Many genres do well on this platform, and Amazon offers great promotions to put your book in front of more readers.

Publishing "wide" means that your e-book is not exclusive to Amazon but available on any platform you choose (which still includes Amazon). This path will put you in front of readers all over the world, as many countries don't have access to Amazon. The big players in a wide-strategy are Amazon, Apple Books, Kobo, B&N, and Google Play.

When making this decision for *The Life After* series, initially I wanted to go into KDP Select. There are authors killing it on that platform who make consistent money. But after reading 'Wide for the Win' by Mark Leslie Lefebvre, I changed my mind. While a wide strategy takes a while to grow an audience, it's a long-term tactic that keeps you in control. You will diversify your income and make your books available to a wider audience around the world.

There's no right or wrong answer here, but I would recommend that if you want to try out KDP Select, you do so initially before going wide. Amazon is strict on their rules that you cannot publish elsewhere, so if you are moving from a wide strategy to KDP Select, then you better comb the internet for any e-book copies available on other websites before enrolling or you risk breaking the terms and conditions of the program.

Note, if you are enrolled in the KDP Select program, you can publish any other formats of the book such as print and audio wide, so that is available if you want to try out KDP Select for your e-books.

Decisions with going Wide

No matter which path you choose, there are different ways that you can upload your book to retailer websites based on many factors.

Uploading Direct

Advantages to uploading direct to book platforms include special promotions and customizable features that are only available on each platform.

Amazon

Amazon has a high royalty rate for direct publishing at 70% (As long as you price your book between $2.99-$9.99 USD). If you are going to direct publish to one platform, this is the one.

Apple Books

You can include a custom sample of your book (not

necessarily the first pages of the book as on other platforms). This option gives you the choice to reveal an exciting part of the book to entice readers to buy.

For giveaways, you can request up to 250 promotional codes per e-book.

Barnes & Noble

You have direct access to a promotions section on the website not available unless you are direct.

Like Apple Books, you can include a custom sample of your book.

Google Play

You can have up to three promotional campaigns per month, and with each campaign you can have up to 5,000 promotional codes. The three types of campaigns are Free, Percentage off (e-books only), and a Fixed price. You can set a promotional price for either multiple books or individual books.

If you have an early review team or street team, in your pre-order stage, you can send copies to content reviewers by simply adding their email address.

Kobo

Like Amazon, Kobo Writing Life offers 70% royalties on e-books priced at $2.99 USD and above.

Like B&N, you have access to internal promotions on the Kobo Writing Life website.

.　.　.

The main disadvantage to uploading direct to each platform is your time. First of all, you have to learn every platform, and they are different when it comes to how they list categories and keywords, and you have to tailor your book to each of them. Uploading more of your books will come easier, but say you want to update your files in the future? You have to go to each of the vendors to change those files, which can take a lot of time, especially the more you publish.

More specific to Apple Books, you will need a Mac to upload through iTunes Producer. A lot of authors who use PC's purchase refurbished Macs for this reason.

Your Website

Outside of the book retailers, you can publish wide from your website storefront. These advantages include earning 80-90% royalties (depending on the transactional fees of your chosen platform), you make income immediately upon purchase, and you have direct customer contact.

The main disadvantages of selling from your website can be the cost of the platform/storefront, and that those sales won't count toward ranking, or bestseller lists on online book retailers.

Uploading with a Distributor

If you would prefer to use a distributor, this will save you time, but will cost you money in either a commission-based payment (where they take a percentage of the royalties) or set payment per month. The more well-known options are:

· · ·

IngramSpark

Cost: Per upload. It varies depending on if you are uploading e-book, print, or both. Many author groups or a quick Google search will find you discount codes or free uploads for IngramSpark.

Distribution: Libraries, global retailers, Barnes & Noble, and the major e-book retailers including Amazon, Apple Books, Kobo, and more. It's worth noting that for distribution to Amazon and Apple books, you'll need to sign an additional addendum.

Smashwords

Cost: They take a commission on all net sales. You earn 60% from major e-book retailers, and up to 80% list on the Smashwords store.

Distribution: Global reach to major retailers and public libraries, and the major e-book retailers including Apple Books, Kobo, B&N, and more.

Draft2Digital

Cost: Commission based. After a book is sold, they take 10% of the retail price.

Distribution: Global distribution to retailers, libraries, and the major e-book retailers including Amazon, Apple Books, Kobo, B&N, and more.

PublishDrive

Cost: Start for free, pay as you grow with a set monthly price.

Distribution: Global distribution to retailers, libraries,

and the major e-book retailers including Amazon, Apple Books, Kobo, B&N, Google Play and more.

Another advantage of using a distributor gives you a wider network of bookstores for your books to appear in. Many of the distributors involve Overdrive and Hoopla, which offer books to libraries. Some of the e-book retailers that are available from the distributor don't have a direct upload feature, so if you want to get your book there, then you have to go with one of them. For instance, at the time of this writing, if you want to publish on Apple Books, but don't have access to a Mac, you will have to go through an aggregator.

As I mentioned promotions in the last section, there are promotions that are available if you publish through a distributor, but that depends on which one you choose.

The most obvious disadvantage is the commission/payment to these companies. It makes sense that they would take a cut or payment since they are providing a service, but it depends on you weighing the benefits of time and money. When using a distributor, there can be payment and uploading/change delays. The distributor has to get paid from the retailer and then take their cut before passing the money to you. Also, if you upload changes to your book files, there may be a delay before the changes appear at the stores (i.e. cover change). Some stores allow you to schedule a price change ahead of time for a sale, so I would take advantage of that so there isn't any pushback from readers when you promote a sale.

Going Hybrid

So what is the "best" way to distribute your book wide? Why not take advantage of both uploading direct and with a distributor?

With a wide publishing mindset, your long-term goal is to get your books in as many readers hands as possible, while making the most of your time, and earning as much from royalties as you can. It's a lot to balance and there isn't a "right" way to do this. To diversify, identify the areas your distributors can reach that are beyond the areas you can direct publish to.

Affiliate Programs

In the vein of making money, affiliate programs offer a great way to make passive income. Affiliate marketing is when you earn a commission by promoting products from a brand or company. For instance, if you were a part of Amazon's affiliate program, and linked your book directly to their store, you could earn a percentage of that sale. You're already publishing in these stores, and offering book links to readers, why not take advantage of these programs to earn more?

Some companies that have affiliate programs are:

- Apple Books Performance Partners
- Google Books
- Amazon Associates
- Kobo
- IngramSpark
- Smashwords
- Draft2Digital
- Bookshop.org

Marketing

A common misconception of having a publisher is that they will do the marketing for you. Many authors fall for this idea early in their careers. Initially, we can be happy to pay for blog tours, swag, and promotion of our books with little help from the publisher. We learn quickly that we have to do most of the work ourselves or see little return.

Now that you have your book back, you have an infinite amount of time to promote it. It's yours, you can change the pricing at any time, run sales, make the first book in your series free, whatever!

The traditional publishing strategy of focusing on releases and then hearing nothing of promotion after your "season" is over no longer holds true. By any means, hold a marketing strategy for your release, but if you are interested in selling your book long-term, do what you need to do to get the book in front of new readers. The more readers you get the book out to, the more fans you will find for this book and future ones.

Paid Advertising

The beauty of controlling your rights is that you have full access to your advertising numbers. Anytime my publisher ran ads for me, I didn't have access to the dashboard to see how the sale was doing or if it resulted in sales at all.

Now that you have full access to the dashboard, you can run ads and tweak based on the results of your sales. The control is there, and it's truly a beautiful thing.

The heavy hitters for paid ads at the time of this writing are:

- Amazon Ads (AMS ads)
- Facebook/Instagram Ads. Since Facebook and Instagram are linked, these ads can appear on both platforms as well.
- Bookbub Ads

"Front List Sells Backlist"

Republishing your reverted book gives you the opportunity to re-release that book and to create that buzz around the new release to sell the other books in your catalog.

If this is the only book you have available, that's okay. The best thing you can do for that book is to release another one.

Re-Publishing Your Book – Review And Actionable Steps:

- Set a reminder to check that there are no outstanding editions available online.
- If you wish to link previous Amazon reviews, contact KDP.
- Apply for affiliate programs.
- Decide if you want to publish KDP Select or wide.
- If you choose KDP Select, review the available promotions and mark your calendar with these dates to take full advantage.
- If you choose wide, decide if you want to publish direct, with a distributor, or with a hybrid model.

How do you want to market your book?

- Paid ads
- Sales
- Promotions

Part IV: Long-Term Plans

Long term plans

This section gives you more to think about to keep your books making you money for many years to come.

Considerations are,

- Pen names
- Sub-rights and book formats
- Future reversion plans
- Your author business

Pen names

Should you use a pen name?

This was an internal debate I had for well over a year. Previously, all of my books from many different genres were published under one name. This made it difficult to find my audience and for the online bookstores to get my books in front of the "right" readers. Those who loved my young adult paranormal novels didn't convert to my new adult romance, and it was even more rare that they wanted to read my adult contemporary fiction and vice versa. When my rights were reverted I was given the opportunity to change what I'd done in the past. Instead of publishing everything under the "Katlyn Duncan" brand, I split into two pen names (for now).

Why you might want a pen name

- You're writing in different genres or age ranges.

- You want to keep your personal identity away from your books. Many professionals do this to keep their name from linking with the books they write, or those who don't want their family, friends, and/or colleagues/clients to know they are publishing.

Using a pen name can be as simple or time-consuming as you want. There are some writers who separate all their genres, or bundle their adult under one name and young adult another. Some have websites built per pen name or all pen names listed on one central site. You could create different websites, newsletters, social media accounts, the works! While this would be a perfect way to segment your readers, weigh the cost of your time and effort, or hire someone to manage it.

The way I went felt like a better compromise than where I've been before. My most successful books, my women's fiction novels will remain under my Katlyn Duncan brand, as will my non-fiction (as I've built up a YouTube channel for writers under that name and it makes sense to keep that "brand"), along with any other adult books I publish. As I'm pivoting to adult thrillers with female protagonists, and the conversion from my women's fiction would be better in that direction, then say my young adult books, I'm keeping that name.

For my reverted young adult books, I've gone with a pen name: Katy Duncan. I wanted a connection with the last name as I am using one website, and to appeal to any crossover readers who read in many genres and age ranges to be able to find more of my work. By having the two names, there will be no mistake in the algorithms that those who want Katy Duncan or Katlyn Duncan books will see more of them on their homepage.

Sub-rights and book formats

A writer's book is their baby. With your publisher, you might have even held your book in your hand before. Those at digital-first or digital-only publishers most likely haven't. In my experience, a book release doesn't quite hit you until you can flip through the pages with your words printed on the paper.

Eleven of my published books were in e-book format only. So, when I got my rights back to my debut series, you bet I went out and created a paperback of the series. Of course the formatting was abysmal (even though I spent several hours trying to figure it out in Word), but I wanted to hold my books. When they arrived, it was one of the best moments in my author career. It also put a fire under me to make my books that much better so that others could put the book on their shelves as well.

Self-publishing can be an overwhelming process at first. You don't have to do it all at once, but *you* are the decision maker now and these books will remain in your control for the rest of your life. This isn't a race, but crossing each checkpoint feels so good when you're driving the car.

Listed in the contract with your publisher, there should be a royalty structure based on sub-rights. Those may include paperback, hardcover, audiobook, large print, film rights, translations, etc. Those and more are all the possibilities you can exercise for your book.

Reversion plan for books still with your publisher

I published thirteen books with my publisher prior to moving on with indie-publishing, and I've only had three reverted to me. There are books I'm interested in getting reverted, and there are some that I know won't be available to me for a while since the sales numbers are well above the reversion threshold in those contracts.

If you have other books with your publisher, I encourage you to think about the future of those too, even though reversion might not be available for years to come.

I track my sales through a spreadsheet based on my royalty statement, and also the reversion metrics based on that particular contract. I signed two contracts with a time-based reversion period but one of them has a unit threshold and the other is a monetary threshold.

In that spreadsheet, I'm tracking the reversion date (based on the amount of years from the publication date) how many units are sold (for the former contract) or how much I'm making (for the latter). Even though the reversion period for these books hasn't lapsed yet, this forward thinking allows me to understand when I might get these books back, so I can plan for how I want to re-release them either for sale, as a reader magnet, or to get them off my list as they no longer serve a purpose within my backlist.

Your author business

There are several business practices which aren't necessary for working with a publisher. While you can start a "business" prior to having a contract, there aren't many authors who do.

But if you want to independently publish your books, it makes sense to create an official business, at least it did to me. If this overwhelms you, then you can skip this step and publish on your own with no trouble.

My main reason for creating a business—my own publishing company—is that I wanted my books to have a publishing house next to the publisher in the book records, versus my name. I created Silent Storm Publishing for all of my future books, and while I won't publish other authors' works, when readers look at my books, it's not obvious from the onset that I'm self-published.

If you want to make this a business for yourself, you have to think like one. That includes separating the person from the author, even if you're not using a pen name. Another simple way to do this is separating personal debit and credit cards that you use for day-to-day spending than your author business spending.

Sources that have helped me a lot when it comes to this mindset:

- 'Self-Publisher's Legal Handbook, Second Edition: Updated Guide to Protecting Your Rights and Wallet' by Helen Sedwick
- 'Business For Authors. How To Be An Author Entrepreneur' by Joanna Penn
- Publish and Thrive course from Sarra Cannon

More recommendations are available in my downloadable resources list at katlynduncan.com/resources.

Long-Term Plans – Review And Actionable Steps:

- Decide if you will use a pen name.
- What sub-rights do you want to exercise for your book? (Note: they all don't need to release at once, but keep them in mind to reach different readers).
- What are your plans for reversion for your backlist titles (if applicable)?
- If you wish to revert, mark your calendar for these future dates.

Closing thoughts

Now that you had a crash course in what happens when your book rights are reverted, and what you can do with them, how do you feel? I want you to be honest, because when I was given all the possibilities back with my debut series, I was somewhat giddy, and very overwhelmed. Those and every feeling in-between are valid.

Previously, we had someone take care of us at the publisher, and they didn't always explain all of the steps of the process. A lot goes into publishing a book, but if you intend to grow as an author and keep your books working for you, rights reversion is a way to do that.

You've got this, I know you do, and I can't wait to see what you do with your book.

Author's Note

While acquiring case studies to give you more of an idea how rights reversions work, I came up against several authors who were fearful to speak about this process. That made me pause and reflect.

Most of the time, I try to be open about the process of publishing. There were instances in my career where things didn't feel particularly "right" when it came to the relationship with my publisher. But I rarely recalled these instances to aspiring published authors for fear of making them feel nervous about the process. Honesty is important to me, and to make it in this business you need knowledge of it first.

When I signed my first contract in 2012, there wasn't as much advice out there, or at least I didn't know where to look for it. While I don't regret any time I spent with my publisher, because it made me more of a confident author by working with editors and other publishing professionals, I regret not having a community that I could speak to about assessing the risks and paths of publishing.

Going forward, I will share my story with others, including the good, bad, and ugly with the hopes of creating a strong author community who fights to keep our stories alive for years to come.

This book is a culmination of pulling all the emotions about my rights reversion and what I've learned about making my books work for me again. I hope you gained some knowledge, and at the very least, some confidence in taking back your book, on your terms.

Thank you and your freebie!

Thank you so much for reading 'Take Back Your Book'. If you have a moment, please head over to your favorite book retailer and leave a review. Even a few sentences goes a long way, and I appreciate the support.

Want to download a free checklist for pre-and post-reversion?
Get your free digital/printable reversion checklist at KatlynDuncan.com/Reversionchecklist.

About Katlyn Duncan

Katlyn Duncan is a multi-published author of adult and young adult fiction, and has ghostwritten over forty novels for children and adults. Her young adult alter-ego, Katy Duncan, loves to write paranormal coming of age stories.

When she's not writing, she's obsessing over many (many) television series', and hanging out on YouTube where she shares her writing process and all the bookish things.

Connect with Katlyn and learn more about her writing and publishing process:

Website: www.KatlynDuncan.com

youtube.com/katlynduncanauthor
instagram.com/authorkatlynduncan
bookbub.com/authors/katlyn-duncan
patreon.com/katlynduncan

Acknowledgements

Thanks to the amazing EQ (Sacha, Crys, and Dan) for pushing me to write this book and helping me to shape my first nonfiction textbook. Your friendship and advice is worth more to this Relator then you will ever know.

I'm eternally grateful to Katie Carroll for the one conversation that sparked this idea, and to Julie and Amber for your incredible support as I navigated this process. To the authors who helped by sharing their stories (Madeline, Maggie, Katie, Keri, Kristine, Terri), and those who participated but chose not to be named, I appreciate your willingness to stand up for your books and I'm so happy that I can help share your advice and amazing books with more readers.

To my community and patrons, I'm grateful for your support of all of my writing endeavors.

Resources

For a digital list of these resources, visit
KatlynDuncan.com/Resources

Writer Associations

- The Author's Guild http://www.authorsguild.org/
- The Alliance of Independent Authors http://allianceindependentauthors.org/
- Society of Children's Book Writers and Illustrators (SCBWI) http://scbwi.org/

Editing

- Editorial Freelancers Association (EFA) https://www.the-efa.org/
- ProWriting Aid http://prowritingaid.com/
- Grammarly http://grammarly.com/

Freelance – Editing and Covers

- Fiverr http://fiverr.com/
- Upwork http://upwork.com/

Covers

- Canva https://katlynduncan.com/canva
- Photoshop https://www.adobe.com/products/photoshop.html

ISBN

- United States/ Bowker
  http://myidentifiers.com/
- United Kingdom/ Nielsen
  http://nielsenisbnstore.com/
- Canada https://www.bac-lac.gc.ca/eng/
  services/isbn-canada/Pages/isbn-
  canada.aspx

Formatting

- Adobe InDesign https://www.adobe.com/
  products/indesign.html
- Atticus https://www.atticus.io/
- KindleCreate https://www.amazon.com/
  Kindle-Create
- Vellum https://katlynduncan.com/vellum
- Scrivener https://www.
  literatureandlatte.com/scrivener

Book Distribution

- Kindle Direct Publishing Amazon
  https://kdp.amazon.com
- Apple Books https://itunesconnect.
  apple.com/
- Barnes and Noble Press https://press.
  barnesandnoble.com/
- Bookfunnel http://bookfunnel.com/
- Draft2Digital http://draft2digital.com/
- Google Play https://play.google.com/
  books/publish
- IngramSpark http://ingramspark.com/

- Kobo https://www.kobo.com/us/en/p/writinglife
- Prolific Works http://prolificworks.com/
- PublishDrive http://publishdrive.com/
- Smashwords http://smashwords.com/
- Story Origin http://storyoriginapp.com/

Recommended Reading

- Business For Authors. How To Be An Author Entrepreneur by Joanna Penn
- Self-Publisher's Legal Handbook, Second Edition: Updated Guide to Protecting Your Rights and Wallet by Helen Sedwick
- The Self-Publishing Blueprint by Daniel Willcocks
- Wide for the Win by Mark Leslie Lefebvre

Recommended Courses

- Starting from Zero by David Gaughran https://courses.davidgaughran.com/courses/starting-from-zero
- Publish and Thrive by Sarra Cannon https://www.katlynduncan.com/publishandthrive
- How to Self-Publish Your Book by Jenna Moreci https://www.skillshare.com/user/jennamoreci

Please note: Some of these links are affiliate links. Purchasing through them doesn't add any cost to you, but I get a small commission if you use them. I appreciate the support.